IS-362.A: Multi-Hazard Emergency Planning for Schools

By

Fema

10/31/2013

IS-362.a - Multihazard Emergency Planning for Schools

Lesson 1: Course Overview

Course Goal

Schools have a duty to take care of their students, staff, and faculty. Most schools are very safe places—but for those unthinkable emergency instances, schools need to have a plan to respond.

The goal of this course is to provide you with an understanding of the importance of your school having an emergency operations plan (EOP) and basic information on how an EOP is developed, exercised, and maintained.

Overall Course Objectives

At the completion of this course you should be able to:

- Describe the activities related to the key areas of incident management.
- Describe how the school emergency operations plan (EOP) fits into district, community, and family/personal emergency plans.
- Identify school staff to participate on the school planning team.
- Identify community members who should be on the school planning team.
- Identify natural, technological, and human-caused hazards.
- Identify and assess hazards likely to impact your school.
- Describe each of the components of the traditional EOP.
- Identify the steps to approve and disseminate the school EOP.
- Describe the Incident Command System (ICS) principles and organization.
- Identify the ICS roles included in the school EOP.
- Explain the benefits of training and exercising the school EOP.
- Identify the types of exercises available to exercise the school's plan.
- Describe steps for developing effective exercises.
- Describe how exercise results are used to improve school preparedness efforts.

Why Should Schools Plan for Emergencies?

"It's really hard to convey this to people if they haven't been through an emergency, and the problem with emergencies is that they happen so rarely. Maybe there'll be an emergency once in my professional career, is how quickly they happen. I never really knew that water could rise that fast, and so after we made the decision to dismiss the students into the community, a real important question was, "What happened . . . What happens then?" Should I have sent teachers with them? Will there be community emergency volunteers available to get them home? I mean, in our community we don't bus . . . I mean, only part of our school system is bused, so my kids were walking. So I basically sent my students out into what was a growing emergency situation." *Peter Clark, Principal, Montpelier, VT*

Incident Management

Principal Peter Clark points out why it is important for schools to have a plan and procedures that identify how to be prepared. Preparedness is advanced through incident management activities—prevention, protection, mitigation, response, and recovery.

Importance of Having a Plan

Effective planning is a key component of incident management that helps prevent emergencies from becoming crises. Schools must plan for emergencies because:

- Schools are responsible for ensuring the safety of students and staff.
- Parents and communities are more confident knowing their schools are prepared for an incident.
- Some State laws require emergency planning.
- Benefits of preparedness extend to the home and community.

Benefits of School Emergency Planning

Having a school emergency plan provides benefits to the school and the community by:

- Presenting opportunities to engage the whole community—students, parents, staff, emergency responders, and community members.
- Giving families a basis to develop their own emergency plans.
- Clarifying roles and responsibilities.
- Improving response to an emergency situation to prevent injuries, save lives, and allow for a more rapid return to normal school operations.
- Providing a comprehensive understanding of the hazards the school faces.

An All-Hazards Approach

One of the benefits of planning is developing an understanding of all the hazards that your school may face. This all-hazards approach to planning is important because although the causes of emergencies may differ greatly, the effects are often similar. Using this approach, schools can develop a plan that includes processes and procedures that prepare them to respond effectively to a variety of hazards such as:

- Natural hazards (earthquakes, floods, tornadoes, etc.).
- Technological hazards (hazardous materials accidents, power outages, computer failures, etc.).
- Human-caused hazards (school violence, bullying, criminal acts, etc.).

Comprehensive Plan

Having a comprehensive plan that addresses all possible hazards is important because emergency situations develop quickly and emergency responders may not be available immediately. A comprehensive plan:

- Identifies the steps for managing all phases of an incident—preincident, during the incident, and postincident.
- Explains what to do in an incident and why it is important to do so.
- Describes important constraints (what "must be done") and restraints (what "must not be done").

The Multihazard Emergency Planning for Schools Toolkit contains materials and resources that can help with developing a comprehensive emergency plan.

Lesson Summary

This lesson introduced why it is important to have a comprehensive school emergency operations plan, to save lives and protect property.

In the next lesson, you will learn about being prepared by implementing protective, prevention, and mitigation measures and how to respond and recover if something does happen.

Lesson 2: Understanding Incident Management

Lesson Overview

This lesson presents the areas of incident management and describes what your school can do to be prepared for emergencies. At the completion of this lesson you should be able to:

- Describe the activities related to the key areas of incident management.
- Describe how the school emergency operations plan (EOP) fits into district, community, and family/personal emergency plans.

Planning Considerations

The previous lesson introduced the importance of having a comprehensive emergency operations plan (EOP). In order to develop a comprehensive EOP, your school must consider activities related to the following key areas:

- **Prevention** The capabilities necessary to avoid, prevent, or stop a threatened or actual act of terrorism. For the purposes of the prevention framework called for in PPD-8, the term "prevention" refers to preventing imminent threats.
- **Protection** The capabilities necessary to secure the homeland against acts of terrorism and manmade or natural disasters.
- **Mitigation** The capabilities necessary to reduce loss of life and property by lessening the impact of disasters.
- **Response** The capabilities necessary to save lives, protect property and the environment, and meet basic human needs after an incident has occurred.
- **Recovery** The capabilities necessary to assist communities affected by an incident to recover effectively.

The Incident Management Continuum

The key areas occur and overlap during more than one phase or time period of an incident.

- **Before the incident:** Prevention, protection, and mitigation actions are taken to stop an incident or reduce its impact.

- **During the incident:** Response activities focus on life safety and then the recovery process begins. During this phase, it is critical to continue prevention and protection actions for a related or new incident.
- **Following the incident:** Response and recovery activities include how best to incorporate prevention, protection, and mitigation measures to be better prepared for the next incident.

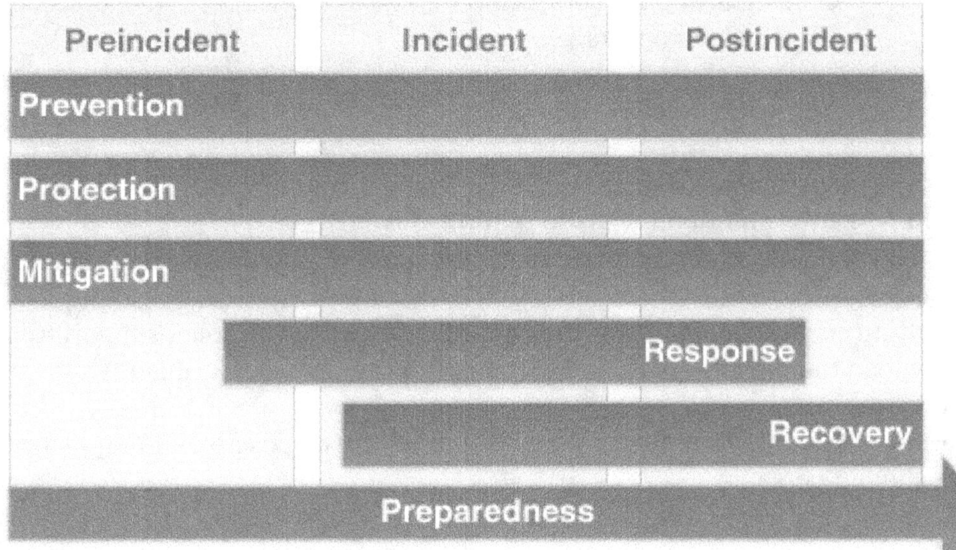

It is important to understand the need to integrate the key areas in your planning efforts during each phase to ensure your school's overall preparedness. The rest of this lesson presents information on what your school can do to address each key area.

Prevention and Protection

During all phases your school needs to consider activities to prevent and protect against hazards and threats. No emergency plan can address every scenario or foresee every outcome. However, a comprehensive planning process can identify potential incidents, and as a result determine prevention and protection measures to stop, minimize, or contain the impact of an incident.

Some examples of prevention and protection measures include:

- Cybersecurity,
- Pandemic influenza sanitation,
- Building access control procedures such as requiring photo IDs, lockdown policies, security systems, and cameras, and
- Site access control.

Mitigation

It is not possible to stop every hazard; for example, your school cannot stop a tornado from occurring. For those hazards that cannot be prevented, your school EOP needs to include ways to reduce their impact. Mitigation measures are ways to save lives and protect property when a hazard occurs.

Some examples of mitigation measures include:

- Securing heavy items to walls;
- Building berms and flood walls to minimize water damage;
- Implementing structural improvements to "harden" school buildings against high winds;
- Installing snow fencing or retrofitting flat roofs with additional support to handle snow load to help save lives and reduce property damage during a winter storm; and
- Cutting vegetation to reduce wild fires and eliminate possible hiding places for threatening persons.

Response

Once an incident happens, your school needs to be prepared to respond quickly and effectively. Response involves:

- Getting emergency equipment in place;
- Getting people out of danger;
- Providing needed food, water, shelter, and medical services; and
- Bringing damaged services and systems back on line.

During response protecting the health and safety of everyone in the school is the first priority, and the protection of property is a second priority.

Response Procedures Characteristics

Your school EOP should include response procedures. These are standardized, specific actions for school staff and students to take for a variety of hazards, threats, or incidents. Response procedures should:

- Encourage clear communication among personnel.

- Be based on National Incident Management System (NIMS)/Incident Command System (ICS) best practices.
- Identify staff responsibilities and duties.
- Include coordination with local fire, law enforcement, and emergency management.
- Be trained and exercised periodically.
- Be updated based on lessons learned from training, exercises, and incidents.

Lesson 5 provides more information on response procedures and Lesson 6 presents details about ICS.

Recovery

As the incident management continuum shows, recovery efforts start when an incident has occurred. The incident may happen quickly, but the recovery process will take time. It is important to plan for recovery, so that it can begin as soon as possible, to help the school cope with the losses and begin to restore structures and operations.

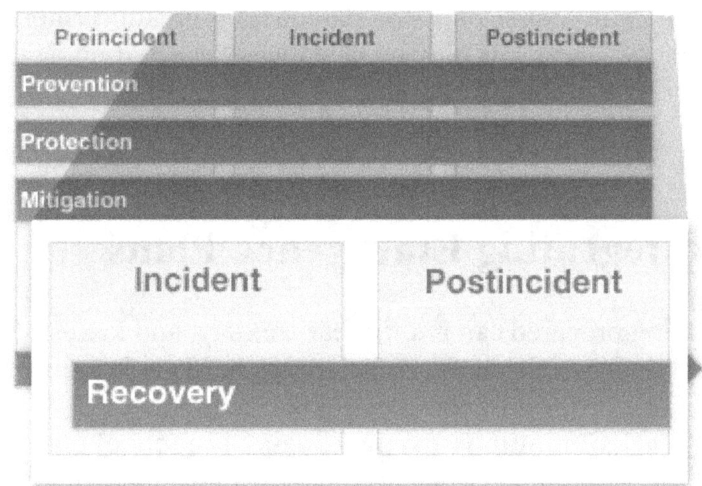

Recovery Procedures

Your school's recovery efforts should include both short-term and long-term procedures for:

- **Academic recovery:** Continue teaching, communicate with parents, and reevaluate the curriculum to determine what topics can be delayed or discarded. The district will need to contact the State department of education to see what flexibility may be available.
- **Physical recovery:** Relocate operations, resume services, obtain equipment, and restore buildings and grounds.

- **Business recovery:** Designate people for decisonmaking, systems for implementing contracts, a system for registering students, and place for redundant records.
- **Emotional and psychological recovery:** Address disruption of school, psychological injury, and pressure from the media.

Preparedness

No emergency plan can address every scenario or foresee every outcome. This lesson has introduced key areas of incident management and what to consider for each area when preparing your EOP. Integrating measures that support prevention, protection, mitigation, recovery, and response will advance your school's overall preparedness.

A part of your school's preparedness is creating emergency kits for classrooms and the school. These kits may be taken when evacuating or stockpiles may be stored to use during a prolonged crisis.

Integrating Emergency Plans

Being prepared can reduce fear, anxiety, and losses of life and property that may accompany incidents. Preparedness needs to happen at all levels, not just the school.

- **Community preparedness:** The school plan must be integrated with the community plan through planning and exercising in collaboration with local emergency management representatives and first responders. This coordination will enable the school to know when and how they will receive assistance from first responders and the school's role in the event of an incident (e.g., a shelter facility for affected residents, a staging area, a point of distribution for emergency supplies and food, etc.).
- **Personal and family preparedness:** School staff members must take steps in advance to ensure the safety of their families, so they can focus on the needs of the school population when an incident occurs. In fact, some States have laws or mandates requiring personnel to remain at their school assignments during an emergency.

Emergency Operations Plan

Developing an emergency operations plan (EOP) is an important part of school preparedness. To provide schools with a process to develop a comprehensive EOP, this training follows the planning steps identified in the Comprehensive Preparedness Guide (CPG) 101:

- **Step 1: Form a collaborative planning team.** In this step your school identifies team members to participate in the planning process.
- **Step 2: Understand the situation.** In this step the planning team identifies possible hazards and threats and determines which ones merit special attention.
- **Step 3: Determine goals and objectives.** In this step the planning team identifies the goals and objectives for school EOP.
- **Step 4: Plan development.** This step is a process of generating, comparing, and selecting possible solutions for achieving the goals and objectives.
- **Step 5: Plan preparation, review, and approval.** This step involves the planning team writing the plan. Then the plan is reviewed, approved, and disseminated.
- **Step 6: Plan implementation and maintenance.** This step includes conducting training to prepare for the tasks identified in the plan and conducting exercises to test the plan.

Lesson Summary

You now know that planning is a key component of preparedness to ensure that your school can:

- Protect against or prevent an incident from occurring,
- Mitigate the impact of an incident, and
- Respond and recover if an incident occurs.

In the next lesson you will learn about the importance of having a team to develop and manage the school emergency operations planning process.

Lesson 3: Forming the Planning Team

Lesson Overview

Planning is the key to the development of an effective emergency operations plan (EOP). The school EOP benefits from active participation of all stakeholders. A planning team with diverse members can help ensure that nothing is overlooked. At the completion of this lesson you should be able to:

- Identify school staff to participate on the school planning team.
- Identify community members who should be on the school planning team.

Step 1: Forming a Collaborative Planning Team

The first step in the planning process is forming a collaborative planning team. Experience and lessons learned indicate that emergency planning is best performed by a team. When working as a team to plan, the team members:

- Better understand the roles played by each team member.
- Build or expand relationships with each other.
- Can generate support and backing of the school chief executive, school board, and other community stakeholders.

Your school planning team should start with a smaller group of planners that is inclusive but not too large to inhibit productivity—the core planning team. The team is later expanded to include more members of the community to provide specific expertise and to review the plan.

Core Planning Team: Valuable Knowledge and Expertise

Begin the selection of core planning team members by identifying school staff that bring knowledge and expertise from their positions to the planning process. Consider including the following personnel on your core planning team:

- Science teachers with knowledge of area weather hazards or hazardous materials in or near the school.
- The school nurse with knowledge in first aid, triage techniques, and the medical needs of the students.

- Special education teachers with knowledge about the functional needs of the school's students with disabilities.
- English teachers and the school newspaper advisor, with experience in dealing with the media.
- The school technology director to identify ways to secure school records.
- The school security director to identify potential security risks and best practices in response.
- The school counselor to help with identifying resources to address psychological trauma.
- Maintenance or facility personnel to identify hazardous materials and safe evacuation routes.

Note: This is not a complete list. Your school may include other personnel on the core planning team.

Identifying Core Planning Team Members

After identifying staff with the necessary expertise, look for those staff that also:

- Have the ability, commitment, authority, and resources to carry out planning responsibilities.
- Agree upon the planning purpose and process.
- Possess good communication skills.
- Have the trust and confidence of colleagues.

Expanding the Planning Team

After the core planning team has conducted some initial planning, or when it is time to review the plan, the team should be expanded to include community members with additional expertise. When selecting expanded team members, the school should look for persons or organizations that have access to information or subject-matter expertise about threats, hazards, and emergency procedures, for example:

- Local/county emergency management.
- Parent-teacher organization member.
- Student council/government member.
- First responders.
- Public health services.
- School risk management or insurance carrier.
- Utility company personnel.
- Local business and industry personnel.

- State education association and union members.
- Voluntary agencies in the community.
- Attorney from school district.

It is important that your school identifies who reviews and who approves the plan, because not every planning team member is an approver. Your State and/or school district may have laws or policies specifying who must review and approve the school's EOP.

Developing an EOP

Once you have identified the planning team, they can start developing a comprehensive all-hazards emergency operations plan (EOP). This course describes a traditional functional EOP format that includes the following components:

- Basic plan
- Functional annexes
- Hazard-specific annexes

Lesson Summary

This lesson presented guidance on selecting members for your school planning team.

Remember that planning is best when performed by a team that includes school and community members.

In the next lesson you will learn about assessing the potential hazards in and around your school.

Lesson 4: Understanding the Situation

Lesson Overview

A school emergency operations plan must address all potential significant hazards—natural, technological, or human-caused. Your planning team members conduct research to identify the school and community hazards and assess the risk of those hazards to determine actions and resources to include in your school EOP. At the completion of this lesson you should be able to:

- Identify natural, technological, and human-caused hazards.
- Identify and assess hazards likely to impact your school.

Step 2: Understanding the Situation

Now that the school planning team has been identified, the next step in the planning process is for the planning team to understand the hazards the school faces by:

- Conducting research and analysis to identify hazards and threats related to the school and community.
- Assessing the risk of those hazards and threats to identify ones that merit special attention, actions that must be planned for, and resources that are needed.

Conducting Research

To understand the situation, the school planning team starts by conducting research and analysis on the school's threats and hazards. Many sources of information exist to assist the planning team in their research efforts, such as:

- Existing emergency plans and reports, such as community EOPs and previous hazard analyses.
- Internet research.
- Local newspaper archives and historical society records.

Using Local Experts

Local experts are another source of information on hazards and threats.

- Building code inspection and enforcement officers.
- Emergency management, fire personnel, and law enforcement personnel.
- Local planning and zoning commissions.
- Local realtors' associations.
- Local public works departments and utilities.
- Flood insurance representatives.
- The Chamber of Commerce.
- Local organizations (e.g., the local chapter of the American Red Cross).
- School board of education attorney.

Types of Hazards

As the school planning team researches the hazards and threats in and around the school, they will consider each type of hazard that is relevant to the school, community, and neighborhood:

- Natural hazards
- Technological hazards
- Human-caused hazards

Identifying Natural Hazards

Natural hazards tend to occur repeatedly in the same geographical locations because they are related to weather patterns and/or physical characteristics of an area. Examples of natural hazards include:

- Avalanche: a mass of snow, ice, and other material that breaks free to move down a slope.
- Drought: a period of drier-than-normal conditions that results in water-related problems.
- Earthquake: a sudden fault slip in the earth's crust.
- Floods: occur when there is more precipitation to a drainage basin than can be readily absorbed or stored within the basin.
- Hurricane: a tropical storm with winds over a constant speed of 74 miles per hour.
- Influenza Pandemic: an outbreak of a contagious disease that spreads rapidly and widely.
- Landslide: the movement of a mass of rock, debris, or earth down a slope.

- Thunderstorm: produces lightning and lightning is unpredictable; it can strike as far as 10 miles from any rainfall.
- Tornado: a funnel-shaped storm cone with winds up to 300 miles per hour.
- Tsunami: a giant wave produced by underwater movement due to earthquakes, volcanic eruptions, landslides, and meteorites.
- Volcano: when a volcano erupts molten rock is expelled through an opening or vent in the earth's surface.
- Wildfire: a raging conflagration that rapidly spreads out of control in the outdoors.
- Winter storm: hazardous winter weather due to various elements such as heavy snow, sleet, or ice accumulation from freezing rain.

Identifying Technological Hazards

Technological hazards often come with little or no warning. They originate from technological or industrial accidents, infrastructure failures, or certain human activities. Technological hazards can cause the loss of life or injury, property damage, social and economic disruption, or environmental degradation.

Examples include:

- Airplane crash.
- Communications and/or computer database failure.
- Dam failure.
- Hazardous materials release.
- Power failure.
- Radiological release.
- Train derailment.
- Urban fire.

Identifying Human-Caused Hazards

Human-caused hazards arise from deliberate, intentional human actions to threaten or harm the well-being of others. It is important for planners to account for the adaptive risk characteristics of human-caused hazards because perpetrators can take steps to identify and circumvent prevention, protection, and mitigation efforts. Because these hazards can change, the planning team must include an ongoing process to evaluate and revise the plan for human-caused hazards. Examples include:

- Bullying and cyberbullying.
- Harassment, including sexting.

* School violence.
* Terrorist act.
* Sabotage.
* Sex offenders.
* Civil disturbance.
* Illegal drugs, including the production, sale, and use of illegal drugs.

Identifying School, Community, and Neighborhood Hazards

Now that you know types of hazards that could impact your school, the next step is to identify specific hazards in your:

* School,
* Neighborhood, and
* Community.

Identifying Hazards—Classrooms, School Building, and School Grounds

Your school planning team, teachers, administrators, and other staff review the school physical infrastructure (classrooms, school grounds, and school buildings) looking at:

* **Structural elements** include any component of the building whose primary function is to support the dead load (e.g., building, roof).
* **Nonstructural elements** include any portion of the building not connected to the main structure (e.g., bookshelves, file cabinets, furnishings).

Checklists can be used to help track items identified.

Identifying Hazards—School Operations

School operations should be reviewed to identify potential hazards:

* On evacuation routes,
* On school bus routes,
* At special events, and
* On field trips.

Identifying Hazards in Your Neighborhood

Your planning team will also consider the surrounding neighborhood to identify hazards and threats, including:

- Transport or storage of hazardous materials (gas stations, truck routes, etc.).
- Dangerous intersections or roads.
- Criminal activity in the neighborhood.
- Registered sex offenders in neighborhoods near school bus stops.
- Risks associated with popular student locations off campus.

Identifying Hazards in Your Community

Your planning team will also consider the surrounding community to identify hazards and threats, including:

- Weather- or geological-related concerns.
- Commercial/industrial facilities (utilities, power lines, and/or industrial facility).
- Transportation corridors (routes used by hazardous materials vehicles).
- Crime levels.

Considering Additional Factors

As the planning team researches the hazards, they need to consider additional factors related to the hazards.

- **Cascading events.** What other hazards may happen as the result of the initial hazard (e.g., earthquake causing explosions at nearby plants)?
- **Special events.** What if the hazard occurs when the school is holding a special event (e.g., football game, graduation, school play)?
- **Off-campus activities.** What if some students and staff are off campus when the hazard occurs?
- **Functional needs of staff and students.** How will the hazard impact those staff and students with functional needs?

Assessing Your Hazards

Once the planning team has identified school, neighborhood, and community hazards, it begins the assessment process to determine which hazards should be addressed in the school plan, what actions must be planned for, and what resources are likely to be needed.

To begin the assessment process, the planning team assesses each hazard. Three commonly used categories for assessment are:

- **Probability**—frequency of occurrence.
- **Time**—how fast the hazard or threat can impact the public.
- **Consequences**—the impact or damage expected.

Addressing the Hazards

After assessing the hazards to identify those of concern, the planning team determines strategies that can be used to:

- Prevent the hazard,
- Protect against the hazard, or
- Mitigate the impact of the hazard.

Lesson 2 introduced the concepts of prevention, protection, and mitigation. The first priority for the school is to stop something from happening through prevention and protection measures. If something does happen, the school needs to have implemented measures and include procedures in the EOP to lessen the impact on life and property.

Protecting Against and Preventing School Violence

School violence is an example of a human-caused hazard that schools can prevent and protect against through:

- Conflict mediation programs.
- Intervention for troubled students.
- Anti-bullying campaigns and training.
- School security systems.
- Partnerships with local law enforcement.

Mitigating School Building Hazards

Mitigation measures for school buildings vary in effort and expense, although they can address both structural and nonstructural hazards.

Structural Measures

- Using fire-retardant materials
- Elevating structures above the floodplain
- Removing unnecessary overhanging structures
- Constructing safe rooms

Nonstructural Measures

- Anchoring bookcases
- Securing overhead fixtures
- Placing shatter-resistant film on windows
- Cutting vegetation back

Lesson Summary

This lesson presented guidance on identifying and assessing the potential hazards at your school.

In order to develop an effective emergency operations plan that will work in all situations, you must consider all potential hazards that could conceivably impact your school.

In the next lesson you will learn how the analysis of hazards helps planners develop the EOP.

Lesson 5: Developing the Plan

Lesson Overview

Emergency operations plans (EOPs) define the scope of preparedness and incident management activities necessary for your school. A complete EOP provides an overview of the school's preparedness and response strategies and includes annexes to describe specific procedures.

Developing a comprehensive EOP includes preparation, review, and approval. At the completion of this lesson you should be able to:

- Describe each of the components of the traditional emergency operations plan (EOP).
- Identify the steps to approve and disseminate the school emergency operations plan (EOP).

Planning Steps

The previous lesson described the first two steps in the planning process: form a planning team and understand the situation. This lesson describes CPG steps 3, 4, and 5:

- Determine goals and objectives for the plan,
- Develop the plan, and
- Prepare, review, and approve the plan.

Determining Goals

Once the school planning team has identified and analyzed the school hazards, they are ready to prepare goals for the school EOP. These goals:

- Address what the school will do when something happens.
- Ensure the plan focuses on identified priorities.
- Are used to determine if the plan is effective.

Sample EOP Goal Statements

Protect the safety and well-being of students and staff.

- Promote a culture of preparedness so that students and staff know what to do in an emergency.
- Establish command and control of an emergency situation until first responders arrive.
- Communicate effectively with parents before, during, and after an emergency.
- Restore academic programs and services as soon as possible after an emergency.
- Provide crisis support to students and staff after an emergency situation.
- Identify and implement lessons learned following an emergency.

Developing the Plan

After developing plan goals, the planning team:

- Reviews the identified hazards,
- Develops alternatives to address each hazard, and
- Recommends the best solution.

The result of this step is an outline for the school's EOP.

Preparing the Plan

With an outline of what the plan should include, the planning team begins the process of writing the plan. This lesson will describe preparing, reviewing, and approving the traditional functional EOP, which includes:

- The **basic plan:** Describes expected hazards, outlines roles and responsibilities, and explains how the school keeps the plan current.
- The **functional annexes:** Describe procedures and missions for many hazards.
- The **hazard-specific annexes:** Describe strategies for managing specific hazards.

Writing a Simple and Clear Plan

The school EOP should be written:

- In plain English,
- Without jargon,
- With minimal use of acronyms,
- With short sentences, and
- In active voice.

The EOP should provide detail that is appropriate to the target audience and the likelihood of the situation. It should also provide guidance for carrying out common tasks as well as enough insight into intent and vision so that responders can handle unexpected events. Plans written for schools with high staff turnover may require additional detail, including small maps, flowcharts, or checklists.

Making the Plan User-Friendly

Identifying the necessary sections and contents is only one part of developing the school EOP. Plans must also be written to be user-friendly. School administrators and staff are more likely to use a plan when information is organized logically and easy to read.

Ensure that the school EOP is:

- **Organized.**
    - Can users find what they need?
    - Is all the information relevant?
    - Is the plan formatted clearly?
    - Is the content presented clearly?
- **Sequenced correctly.**
    - Can users understand the rationale for the sequencing?
    - Are users able to scan for information they need?
- **Consistent.**
    - Does each section use the same logical progression, or do users have to reorient themselves?
- **Adaptable and compatible.**
    - Is the information easy to use during unanticipated situations?
    - Can the information be applied or adapted to effectively respond to each unique situation?
    - Does the format promote or hinder coordination with local response agencies and personnel?

Basic Plan

Now that you have some strategies for writing the school EOP, let's look at the elements of the basic plan.

Purpose, Scope, Situation Overview, and Assumptions

The Concept of Operations

Organization and Assignment of Responsibilities

Direction, Control, and Coordination

Communications

Administration, Finance, and Logistics

Plan Development and Maintenance

Authorities and References

The next part of this lesson provides details on what should be included in each element of your school's basic plan.

Basic Plan Outline

1. Basic Plan

   a. Introductory Material
      i. Promulgation Document/Signature Page
      ii. Approval and Implementation
      iii. Record of Changes
      iv. Record of Distribution
      v. Table of Contents
   b. Purpose, Scope, Situation Overview, and Assumptions
      i. Purpose
      ii. Scope
      iii. Situation Overview
            a. Hazard Analysis Summary
            b. Capability Assessment
            c. Mitigation Overview
      iv. Assumptions
   c. Concept of Operations
   d. Organization and Assignment of Responsibilities
   e. Direction, Control, and Coordination

f. Information Collection and Dissemination
g. Communications
h. Administration, Finance, and Logistics
i. Plan Development and Maintenance
j. Authorities and References

Purpose, Scope, Situation Overview, and Assumptions

The first element of the basic plan, **Purpose, Scope, Situation Overview, and Assumptions**, provides a rationale for the development, maintenance, and implementation of the school EOP. It includes four components:

<table>
<tr><td>Purpose, Scope, Situation Overview, and Assumptions</td></tr>
</table>

- **Purpose of the Plan** is a general statement of what the EOP is meant to do.
- **Scope of the Plan** outlines the scope of the school's emergency and disaster response and includes:
    - A brief description of the school's response to incidents.
    - The entities (staff, superintendent, local government, etc.) with roles and responsibilities outlined in the plan.
    - The geographic areas covered in the plan, specifically school buildings and grounds.
- **Situation Overview** explains why an EOP is necessary and summarizes the hazards faced by the school. The situation section covers:
    - The geographical and political jurisdiction of the school.
    - A brief synopsis of local hazards and past incidents.
    - A summary of potential, wide-reaching threats to the school community, such as pandemic flu.
    - Relative probability and impact of the hazards.
    - Geographic areas likely to be affected by particular hazards.
    - Vulnerable critical facilities (infrastructure, etc.).
    - Population distribution.
    - Characteristics and locations of populations with functional needs.
- **Planning Assumptions** are what the core planning team assumed to be facts for planning purposes. Obvious assumptions should be included but limited to those that need to be explicitly stated. For example, do not state as an assumption that the hazard will occur; it is reasonable for the reader to believe that if the hazard was not possible, the plan would not address it.

Concept of Operations (CONOPS)

The Concept of Operations (CONOPS) section explains in broad terms the intent of the EOP. The CONOPS presents a clear picture of the sequence and scope of the planned emergency response, what should happen, when, and at whose direction.

- Emergency plan goals.
- Division of responsibilities.
- Sequence of actions—before, during, and after the incident.
- Requesting resources—who can request, who will fill them, how additional aid will be requested.
- An overview of:
  - Direction and control activities,
  - Alert and warning processes, and
  - Continuity of operations (COOP) matters.

Organization and Assignment of Responsibilities

The Organization and Assignment of Responsibilities section establishes an operational organization that is charged to respond to all hazards. It includes a list of tasks to be performed by position and organization.

Although the primary purpose of the EOP is incident management, your school's EOP may identify preincident roles and responsibilities for prevention, protection, and mitigation activities.

- **Preincident** (prevention, protection, and mitigation) roles
  - **Intelligence/Information Gatherer:** Conduct hazard analysis.
  - **Policy Maker:** Develop policies and procedures to reduce risks.
  - **Planner:** Develop and maintain the EOP.
  - **Marketer/Communicator:** Sell the concept of prevention, protection, and mitigation.
  - **Trainer:** Develop and implement training and exercises.
  - **Financer:** Identify the cost/benefit of implementing prevention, protection, and mitigation measures.
  - **Evaluator:** Identify best practices and lessons learned.

Incident Management Roles and Responsibilities

The Organization and Assignment of Responsibilities section should also describe incident management roles. These should be filled by school personnel and/or first responders based on the event or incident and the organization with the authority and expertise to manage the incident. These roles and responsibilities align with the National Incident Management System (NIMS) for better coordination with first responders, law enforcement, and emergency management officials.

- **Incident management** (response and recovery) roles
  - **Senior Executive (Superintendent, Principal, Emergency Management Official, Elected Official, etc.):** Provides policy guidance on priorities and objectives based on situational needs and the school EOP. **Oversees resource coordination and support to the Incident Commander.**
  - **Incident Commander:** Sets the incident objectives, strategies, and priorities and has overall responsibility for the incident.
  - **Public Information Officer:** Serves as the conduit for information to internal and external stakeholders, including the media or other organizations seeking information directly from the incident or event.
  - **Liaison Officer:** Serves as the primary contact for supporting agencies assisting at an incident.
  - **Safety Officer:** Monitors safety conditions and develops measures for assuring the safety of all assigned personnel.
  - **Operations Section Chief:** Establishes the tactics to meet the incident objectives and directs all operational resources.
  - **Planning Section Chief:** Supports the incident action planning process by tracking resources, collecting/analyzing information, and maintaining documentation.
  - **Logistics Section Chief:** Provides resources and needed services to support the achievement of the incident objectives.
  - **Finance and Administration Section Chief:** Monitors costs related to the incident. Provides accounting, procurement, time recording, and cost analyses.

Lesson 6 presents more information on NIMS and the Incident Command System (ICS).

Direction, Control, and Coordination

The Direction, Control, and Coordination section of the basic plan outlines the ways in which schools will coordinate with outside agencies and how the school EOP fits into other, related EOPs.

It is important that the school planning team coordinates with local law enforcement, fire, and emergency management to develop a plan that operates in conjunction with other local community EOPs.

- Explains how:
  - ICS will be implemented.
  - The school will coordinate with local fire, law enforcement, and emergency management.
  - The school EOP fits into the larger community and State EOP.

Communications

The Communications section of your school EOP describes a strategy for informing school staff and students of what is happening and what to do during an emergency, and also for communicating with persons outside the school building regarding an emergency situation.

- Describes communication:
  - **Internally:** Between the school, staff, and students.
  - **Externally:** To parents, responders, school board members, and the media.

Examples of External Communications Activities

The Communications section identifies strategies for external communication—with parents, the media, school board, and emergency responders.

Before an incident your school should:

- Conduct outreach to explain the EOP and describe procedures to parents.

- Identify a Public Information Officer as a single point to communicate with the media and to control rumors and develop standard templates for statements to the media.
- Develop partnerships with parent volunteers for assistance during an incident.
- Identify systems that will be used to provide communication.
- Develop procedures with emergency responders for transferring command.
- Identify communication systems that work within the school and with other agencies.

During an incident your EOP should describe how and when to activate communication systems that provide information to parents.

Following an incident your school may work with parents and emergency responders to identify lessons learned and next steps.

Administration, Finance, and Logistics

Administration, Finance, and Logistics

- The **Administration** section describes:
  - The actions taken to document information and actions during and after the incident.
  - Reasons for documentation (e.g., insurance, recover costs, etc.).
  - After-action report process.
- The **Finance** section describes how, during an emergency operation, your school will:
  - Recover costs.
  - Document costs.
- The **Logistics** section describes:
  - How your school will identify and acquire resources before an emergency.
  - Specialized equipment, facilities, personnel, and emergency response organizations currently available to the school.
  - Agreements and contracts with organizations to supply needed resources.

Note: To support the Logistics section, the school should maintain (e.g., in an appendix to the school plan or as a separate document) a list of the types of resources available, amounts on hand, locations maintained, and any restrictions on use.

Plan Development and Maintenance

Plan Development and Maintenance

- The **Plan Development and Maintenance** section of your school's EOP describes how the plan will be reviewed and updated, including:
    - How the plan fits into the district and local community plans.
    - The process for reviewing and revising the plan each year.
    - To whom the plan is distributed.
    - A page to document plan changes.

Authorities and References

Authorities and References

- The **Authorities and References** section provides a legal basis for emergency operations and activities and includes lists of laws, statutes, ordinances, executive orders, regulations, and formal agreements relevant to:
    - Emergencies, and the specific extent and limits of the emergency authorities.
    - Preparation of the school EOP.
    - Plan approval, dissemination, and execution.

Note: There may be local, State, or Federal laws and regulations that mandate that schools develop and maintain emergency operations plans.

Functional Annexes

Now that we've reviewed the elements that make up the basic plan, let's focus on the next component of the EOP—functional annexes.

While the basic plan provides overarching information on emergency operations, the functional annexes describe the policies, roles, responsibilities, and processes for a specific emergency function that can be applied to different hazards. For example, parent notification procedures for school closure will be the same for all incidents involving the closing of your school—e.g., inclement weather, pandemic flu, power outage.

Developing Functional Annexes

The planning team identifies the functions that are critical to successful emergency response. These functions become the subjects of separate functional annexes, which describe:

- Situations under which the procedures should be used.
- Who has the authority to activate the procedures.
- Specific actions to be taken when the procedures are implemented.
- Procedures for populations with functional needs and special situations (e.g., off-campus events, and students or staff with functional needs).

Functional annexes fall into three categories: response procedures, continuity of operations (COOP) procedures, and recovery procedures.

Functional Annexes—Response Procedures

Response procedures are standardized, specific actions for school staff and students to take for a variety of hazards, threats, or incidents.

Examples of response procedures to include in your school EOP are:

- Drop, cover, and hold
- Evacuation
- Reverse evacuation
- Shelter-in-place
- Lockdown
- Lockout
- Reunification
- Communications

Developing and practicing response procedures enables school staff and students to quickly and safely react in a variety of situations.

Functional Annexes—Recovery Procedures

Recovery procedures define actions taken that are an extension of the response. Recovery procedures include Continuity of Operations (COOP) procedures that are essential functions taken immediately after an incident when normal operations have been severely disrupted.

Your EOP should include recovery procedures that address:

- Academic recovery
- Physical recovery
- Business recovery
- Emotional and psychological recovery

Academic Recovery Procedures

Strategies for academic recovery include:

- **Continuing instruction,** using such strategies as:
  o Mailing lessons to students.
  o Using telecommunications (e.g., local television or radio stations, text messages, emails, Web portals).
  o Providing tutors for homebound students.
  o Rearranging the syllabus or tests until needed facilities are available.
- **Communicating with parents** regarding changes to schedules, updates on classroom locations, and information on the status of the school building. Keeping parents informed is critical to maintaining their support.
- **Reevaluating the curriculum** and determining what topics can be delayed or discarded. Contact the State department of education to see what flexibility may be available to local school districts.

Physical Recovery Procedures

Physical recovery procedures include:

- **Where to relocate** classrooms and administrative operations. Consider locations for both short-term and long-term operations, and the decisionmaking process for selecting a location.
- **How transportation and food services will resume.** Consider how students will get to the school if an important road is damaged in an incident.
- **How to obtain classroom equipment, books, and materials** in advance of relocating, either to a new temporary or permanent location or moving back to a former, restored location.
- **How to restore buildings and grounds** (e.g., debris removal, repairing, repainting, and/or relandscaping).

Business Recovery

Business recovery procedures should designate:

- **People responsible for making the decision** to close schools, or send students/staff to alternate locations. Identify ways to convey that information to parents, students, school staff, and district officials.
- **Systems for rapid contract execution** after an incident. The period after a school building has been destroyed is not the ideal time to start negotiating contracts on temporary building space.
- **A system for registering students** (out of district or into alternative schools). Displaced students may be missing immunization records, proof of residency, or cumulative folders and permanent school records. If a nearby school district is able to reopen their schools sooner, parents may want to enroll their children in that district.
- **A place to keep redundant records.** Keep important records in another location. Be sure to include a copy of the school's insurance policy, and keep the policy current.
- **A line of succession,** including who is responsible for restoring which business functions for schools/districts. Restore administrative and recordkeeping functions such as payroll, accounting, and personal records.

Emotional and Psychological Recovery

While damage to the infrastructure may be most obvious, medical and psychological issues resulting from the incident may be harder to recognize and more critical to address. The psychological healing annex should address:

- **Disruption of regular school functions.**
- **Psychological injury to students and/or staff.**
- **Pressure from the media.** Reporters may try to interview parents, students, and school personnel after an incident. Schools should provide guidelines on how to handle the media and remind parents and students that they have a right to privacy and are not obligated to talk to the media. A school-appointed media liaison can address media questions and handle any difficulties.

School personnel can facilitate psychological healing among those who have been affected by a school emergency by:

- Providing as much factual information as possible about what has happened and what can be expected in the future (including the stages of grieving, if appropriate).
- Avoiding additional changes to set routines.

- Providing an accepting atmosphere in which students and staff can voice concerns, feelings, and fears.
- Providing outlets for the expression of emotions.

Your school EOP may include provisions for a crisis response team to help in the healing process. The decision to activate and deploy the crisis response team should be included in school EOP procedures.

Crisis Response Teams

After an incident, expect a wide range of grieving behavior—from screaming, displays of anger, sobbing, silence, or being apparently unaffected. Faculty, staff, and administrators are not immune from grief. School personnel should expect and accept grief in whatever forms it takes and encourage the natural expression of grief from all who are affected.

A crisis response team can help in the healing process by:

- **Reducing fear,** including addressing students' fears that the incident may occur again.
- **Facilitating grieving,** including formulating a policy on funerals and other memorials, helping plan incident- and age-appropriate student activities, and obtaining as needed the services of trained counselors and other experts outside the school.
- **Supporting parents,** including answering questions about the incident and school response, and offering advice on addressing children's needs.
- **Promoting education,** including calling in substitute teachers as needed.
- **Planning for postincident response actions,** including identifying and contacting any at-risk students, holding meetings with parents or the community, and revising the school EOP.

Crisis response team members:

- Are trained to handle emotional response issues.
- Have the ability and authority to make decisions.

Members of this team should include the school counselor and others who are:

- Respected within the school and the community.
- Sensitive to student, staff, and community needs.
- Calm and able to make decisions in stressful situations.
- Community mental health professionals.

Hazard-Specific Annexes

We've now reviewed two of the three components of the school's EOP—the basic plan and functional annexes. The last component is hazard-specific annexes.

Hazard-specific annexes describe emergency response procedures for a specific hazard. They focus on the special planning needs generated by the one hazard. For example, your school may have a hazard-specific annex that addresses the unique procedures used to respond to specific hazardous materials used at your school.

Selecting Hazards

To identify hazard-specific annexes, the planning team reviews the hazards they identified (CPG Step 2: Understand the Situation) and identifies any that require unique procedures.

The hazard-specific annex:

- Should not repeat information in the basic plan or functional annexes.
- Is only needed when a hazard presents a unique challenge.
- Includes:
    - Where and how the hazard will impact the school.
    - Planning, mitigation, and response needs for the hazard.
    - Legal requirements directed by local, State, or Federal laws.

Hazard-Specific Annex Examples

Your school may want to include hazard-specific annexes for:

- Pandemic flu,
- Flood,
- Earthquake,
- Hazardous materials, and
- School violence.

Click on each type of hazard for information you can use to create a hazard-specific annex for that hazard.

These are examples of hazard-specific annexes, your school or district may identify others.

CPG 101 Hazard-Specific Annex Content Guide Checklist

These annexes describe emergency response strategies that apply to a specific hazard.

Schools may integrate hazard-specific information into functional annexes if they believe such integration would make the plan easier to read and use. Conversely, the unique functional needs generated by the hazard should be addressed in the hazard/threat annex.

Schools may find it appropriate to address specific hazards or threats in completely separate and stand-alone plans. In this case, the EOP must specifically reference those plans and provide a brief summary of how the EOP is to be coordinated with the stand-alone plans.

Some hazards have unique planning requirements directed by specific State and Federal laws. The local emergency management agency must review those requirements and determine how the EOP can best address and meet those legal requirements.

Human-Caused Hazards

These are disasters created by man, either intentionally or by accident.

- **Civil Unrest**

  This section of the annex should address the hazard-specific methods the school uses to prepare for and respond to civil unrest emergencies/disasters. The section should also identify and describe the school's specific concerns, capabilities, training, agencies, and resources that will be used to mitigate against, prepare for, respond to, and recover from civil unrest emergencies (e.g., riots, school shootings).

- **Terrorism**

  This section of the annex should identify and describe the school's specific concerns, capabilities, training, agencies, and resources that will be used to prevent, protect against, prepare for, respond to, and recover from terrorist acts. The attacks covered should include, but not be limited to, attacks involving weapons of mass destruction, such as CBRNE incidents. **Note:** Some State emergency management agencies or homeland security offices have developed specific guidance for this planning element. Specific planning criteria are established in that guidance, and it must be reviewed in order to develop the terrorism plan. Planners should ensure that the EOP is compliant with any State, territorial, or tribal terrorism planning criteria.

Natural Hazards

- **Biological Incidents**
  This section of the annex should identify and describe the school's specific concerns, capabilities, training, agencies, and resources that will be used to mitigate against, prepare for, respond to, and recover from epidemic diseases and biological incidents (e.g., West Nile virus, hoof and mouth disease, smallpox). Include a hazard analysis summary that discusses where/how biological incidents are likely to impact the school.
- **Droughts**
  This section of the annex should identify and describe the school's specific concerns, capabilities, training, agencies, and resources that will be used to mitigate against, prepare for, respond to, and recover from droughts (e.g., water conservation, public water outages, and wildfire issues). Include a hazard analysis summary that discusses where/how droughts are likely to impact the school.
- **Earthquakes**
  This section of the annex should identify and describe the school's specific concerns, capabilities, training, agencies, and resources that will be used to mitigate against, prepare for, respond to, and recover from earthquakes. Include a hazard analysis summary that discusses where/how earthquakes are likely to impact the school.
- **Flood/Dam Failures**
  This section of the annex should identify and describe the school's specific concerns, capabilities, training, agencies, and resources that will be used to mitigate against, prepare for, respond to, and recover from flood/dam emergencies/disasters (e.g., flash floods, inundation floods, floods resulting from dam failures or ice jams). Include a hazard summary that discusses where (e.g., 100-year and common floodplains) and how floods are likely to impact the school.
- **Hurricanes/Severe Storms**
  This section of the annex should identify and describe the school's specific concerns, capabilities, training, agencies, and resources that will be used to mitigate against, prepare for, respond to, and recover from hurricanes/severe storms. Include a hazard analysis summary that discusses where/how hurricanes/severe storms are likely to impact the school.
- **Tornadoes**
  This section of the annex should identify and describe the school's specific concerns, capabilities, training, agencies, and resources that will be used to mitigate against, prepare for, respond to, and recover from tornadoes. Include a hazard analysis summary that discusses where/how tornadoes are likely to impact the school (e.g., historical/seasonal trends, damage levels F1 through F5).
- **Winter Storms**
  This section of the annex should identify and describe the school's

specific concerns, capabilities, training, agencies, and resources that will
be used to mitigate against, prepare for, respond to, and recover from
winter storms (e.g., blizzards, ice jams, ice storms). Include a hazard
analysis summary that discusses where/how winter storms are likely to
impact the school.

Technological Hazards

These incidents involve materials created by man and that pose a unique hazard to the
general public and environment. The school needs to consider incidents that are caused
by accident (e.g., mechanical failure, human mistake), result from an emergency caused
by another hazard (e.g., flood, storm), or are caused intentionally.

- **Hazardous Materials**
  This section of the annex should address the hazard-specific procedures
  and methods used to prepare for and respond to releases that involve
  hazardous materials that are manufactured, stored, or used at fixed
  facilities or in transport (if not addressed in a functional annex). This
  section may include materials that exhibit incendiary or explosive
  properties when released. **Note:** Some States have laws that require each
  Local Emergency Planning Committee (LEPC) to develop a Chemical
  Emergency Preparedness and Response Plan on this topic. Some States
  have laws requiring the local emergency management agency to
  incorporate the LEPC's plan into the emergency management agency's
  planning and preparedness activities. Specific planning criteria established
  by a State Emergency Response Commission must be reviewed and
  addressed in order to develop the LEPC plan.
- **Lethal Chemical Agents and Munitions**
  This section of the annex should identify and describe the school's
  specific concerns, capabilities, training, agencies, and resources used to
  mitigate against, prepare for, respond to, and recover from lethal chemical
  agent and munitions incidents (e.g., sarin, mustard, and VX). Include a
  hazard analysis summary that discusses where/how chemical agent
  incidents are likely to impact the school.
- **Radiological Incidents**
  This section of the annex should address the hazard-specific methods to
  prepare for and respond to releases that involve radiological materials that
  are at licensed facilities or in transport.
  - Describe/identify the school's specific concerns, capabilities,
    training, agencies, and resources that will be used to mitigate
    against, prepare for, respond to, and recover from radiological
    hazards. Include a hazard analysis summary that discusses
    where/how radiological materials are likely to impact the school,
    including incidents that occur at fixed facilities, along
    transportation routes, or as fallout from a nuclear weapon.

Additional Hazards (as Applicable)
Add additional annexes to include other hazards identified through the school's hazard analysis (e.g., mass casualty, plane crash, train crash/derailment, school emergencies).

- Describe/identify the school's specific concerns, capabilities, training, agencies, and resources that will be used to mitigate against, prepare for, respond to, and recover from other hazards as defined in the school's hazard analysis.

Source: Adapted from Comprehensive Preparedness Guide 101 Version 2.0, November 2010, Appendix C

Reviewing, Approving, and Disseminating the Plan

CPG Step 5 includes writing, reviewing, approving, and disseminating the plan. We have reviewed what to include when writing each of the plan components—basic plan, functional annexes, and hazard-specific annexes. Now let's review what is involved in the other steps:

- Review the plan.
- Obtain plan approval.
- Disseminate the plan.

Review the Plan

After writing the plan, the planning team should review the plan for:

- Adequacy.
    - Does the plan identify critical tasks?
    - Are the plan's assumptions valid and reasonable?
    - Does the plan comply with guidance?
- Feasibility.
    - Does the school have the resources to fulfill the tasks identified in the plan?
    - Does the plan identify where the school will obtain resources outside of the school's capabilities?
- Acceptability.
    - Does the plan thoroughly address the identified hazards and threats?
    - Is the plan consistent with legal requirements?

- Completeness.
  - Does the school plan include all the tasks to be accomplished?
  - Does it address staff and students with functional needs?
  - Does it provide a complete picture of what should happen, when, and at whose direction?
- Compliance.
  - Does the school plan comply with laws and regulations?

Stakeholders To Review and Approve

Once the planning team has reviewed the plan, other stakeholders should be included in the review and approval process. The review and approval process should aim to gain the widest acceptance for the plan and include agencies with emergency or homeland security responsibilities.

Consider the following stakeholders for your review and approval process:

- School district officials/employees
- Local fire departments, law enforcement agencies, and/or emergency management
- Elected officials
- School board members
- State department of education
- State director of homeland security or emergency management
- Public works
- Other State and/or Federal officials

Once approved the EOP should include an approval and implementation page with a delegation of authority, a date, and signature by the senior official.

Disseminate the Plan

Once the plan has been reviewed and approved by stakeholders, the plan should be presented to the appropriate officials for formal promulgation. Then the plan can be distributed.

The school should maintain a record of the people and organizations that received a copy of the plan. "Sunshine" laws may require that a copy of the plan be posted on a Web site or some publicly accessible location; if so, sensitive information should first be removed.

After distribution, the school should include a record of both distribution and changes:

- **Record of distribution:** For each person receiving the plan, record name, title, agency, date of delivery, and number of copies delivered.
- **Record of changes:** For each change, include a record of any changes made including a change number, the date of the change, and the name of the person who made the change.

Lesson Summary

This lesson presented information on developing a comprehensive school emergency operations plan that includes: a basic plan, functional annexes, and hazard-specific annexes. The lesson reviewed the following steps in the process for developing the plan:

- CPG Step 3: Determine Goals
- CPG Step 4: Plan Development
- CPG Step 5: Plan Preparation, Review, and Approval

Lesson 6 provides an overview of the Incident Command System and NIMS.

Lesson 6: Incorporating ICS

Lesson Overview

The Incident Command System (ICS) provides a standardized incident management approach to ensure schools can effectively respond during an emergency and protect the students and staff.

This lesson provides an overview of ICS principles, structure, and roles to enable schools to include ICS in their emergency planning process. At the completion of this lesson you should be able to:

- Describe the ICS principles and organization.
- Identify the ICS roles included in the school EOP.

What Is ICS?

ICS can be used to manage any of the following types of incidents:

- Disasters, such as fires, tornadoes, floods, ice storms or earthquakes.
- Disease outbreaks and prevention measures.
- Search operations for a missing student.
- Hazardous materials accidents in chemistry lab.
- Hostile intruders or other criminal acts.
- Planned events, such as school drills, festivals, sport events, and graduations.

Using ICS

The Incident Command System (ICS) helps to ensure:

- Life safety.
- Property protection.
- Incident stabilization.

Adopting ICS will help school personnel work with emergency responders to provide a coordinated response. ICS is the common link between the school and all others who are involved with (or have an interest in) the incident.

National Incident Management System (NIMS)

The National Incident Management System (NIMS):

- Is a consistent, nationwide approach for all levels of government to work effectively and efficiently together to prepare for and respond to domestic incidents.
- Is a core set of concepts, principles, and terminology for incident command and multiagency coordination.
- Requires the use of the Incident Command System (ICS).

ICS is a condition of receiving Federal preparedness funding and this condition applies to schools receiving emergency preparedness funding including the U.S. Department of Education Readiness and Emergency Management for Schools (REMS) grants, CFDA #84.184 E (formerly known as the Emergency Response and Crisis Management (ERCM) grant program).

ICS Principle: Response Requires Certain Functions

ICS is based on certain principles that have proven successful in managing emergency situations. A fundamental principle is that emergencies require certain tasks or functions to be performed.

For example, every incident will require such functions as student care, site or facility security, and communications.

These functions should be identified during the development of the school's concept of operations and, if possible, personnel should be matched to functions at that time.

ICS Principle: One Person Is in Charge

For every incident it needs to be clear who is in charge. When using ICS, that person in charge is the **Incident Commander** who:

- Has the authority to establish objectives, make assignments, and order resources.
- Works closely with staff and technical experts to analyze the situation and determine strategies.
- Should have training, experience, and expertise to serve in this capacity.

ICS Principle: Chain, Unity, and Transfer of Command

ICS provides for an orderly line of authority. Under ICS, personnel:

- Report to only one person, their ICS supervisor.
- Receive work assignments only from this ICS supervisor.

A clear chain of command eliminates confusion during the stress of an incident.

Command can be transferred from one Incident Commander to another when a more qualified Incident Commander is needed or available or for legal reasons.

ICS Principle: Common Terminology Is Key

During an incident it is critical that everyone can communicate clearly. ICS emphasizes:

- Using common terms or clear text.
- **Not** using radio codes, agency-specific codes, acronyms, or jargon.

ICS Principle: Manageable Span of Control

"Span of control" refers to the number of individuals or resources that one supervisor can manage effectively during an incident. Experience has shown that an effective span of control for a supervisor in an incident is three to seven people.

Fewer than three people generally leads to inefficient operations. Greater than seven is generally too many for one individual to manage during an incident.

The ICS Organization

The ICS organization is unique but easy to understand. It expands or contracts to meet the needs of the incident. The Incident Commander only creates the sections necessary and personally manages those functions that are not staffed.

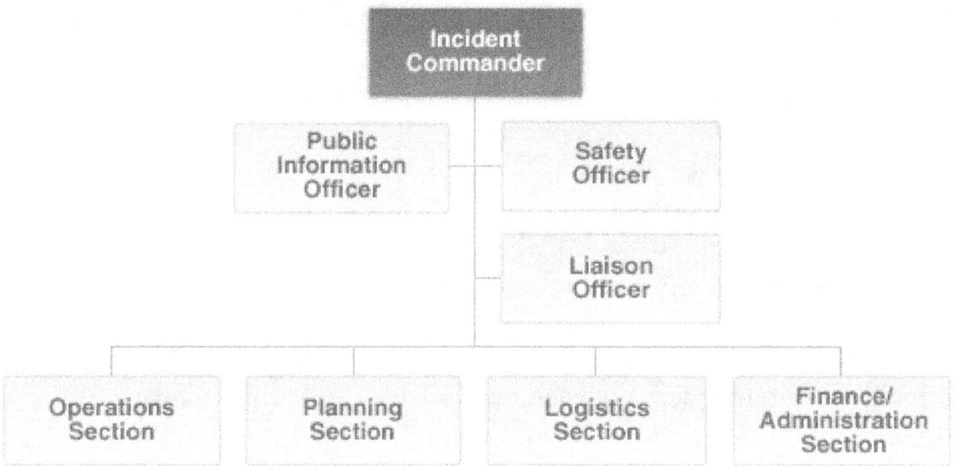

Incident Commander's Responsibilities

In an incident, the Incident Commander manages the entire incident and:

- Assesses the situation.
- Establishes objectives.
- Ensures overall safety.
- Communicates with internal and external stakeholders.
- Organizes resources.
- Develops a strategy or plan for handling the incident, monitors it in process, and adjusts the plan as needed.
- Ensures proper documentation.
- Appoints additional staff as necessary.

Command Staff

The following positions comprise the Command Staff that provide information, safety, and liaison services:

- The **Public Information Officer** is the conduit for information to internal and external stakeholders, including the media.
- The **Safety Officer** ensures that the safety of students, staff, and others on campus is the highest priority and can halt response activities determined as unsafe.

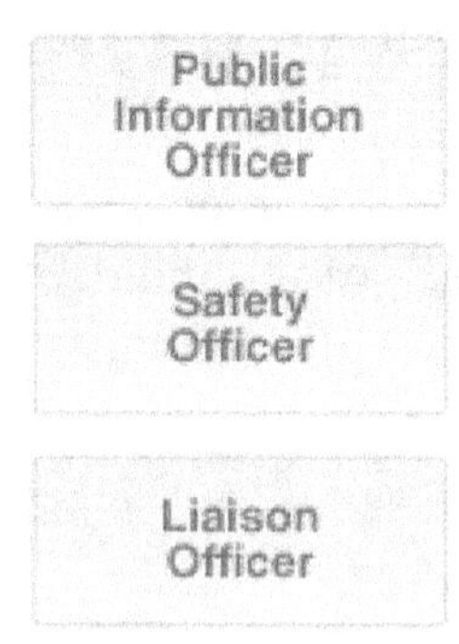

- The **Liaison Officer** coordinates efforts with other agencies assisting at an incident and monitors for any problems between the school and the other agencies.

General Staff

The General Staff perform functional activities:

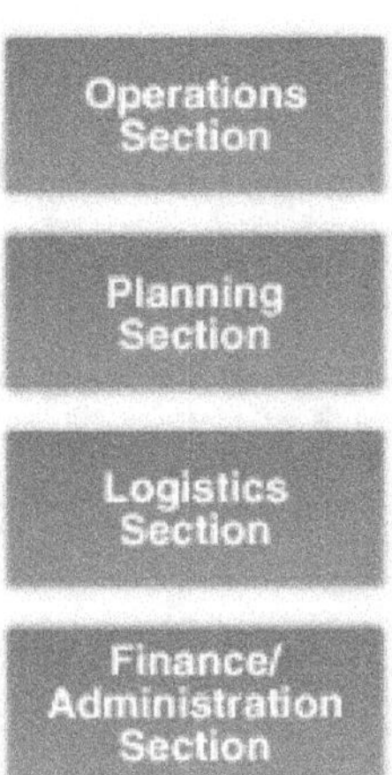

- The **Operations Section** handles all emergency response jobs, including taking care of students. Most adult responders will be assigned jobs in the Operations Section.
- The **Planning Section** supports the incident action planning process by tracking resources, collecting/analyzing information, and maintaining documentation.
- The **Logistics Section** manages resources including supplies, personnel, and equipment.
- The **Finance/Administration Section** monitors costs related to the incident, and provides accounting, procurement, time recording, and cost analyses. (**Note:** A school plan's ICS may not include a Finance/Administration Section. This function may be performed at the school district level. In such circumstances, the Incident Commander must ensure that proper documentation is maintained.)

Possible Assignments in a Disaster

In a major incident or disaster, the following emergency team assignments may need to be established:

- Communications (Logistics)
- Food, Water, and Supply Management (Logistics)
- Medical/First Aid (Operations)
- Maintenance/Fire (Operations)
- Light Search and Rescue (Operations)
- Student Care and Reunification (Operations)
- Student Release (Operations)

- Crisis Response (Operations)

Example of ICS Structure at a School

ICS includes the ability to expand or contract the organization to meet the needs of the situation. The diagram below shows an example of an ICS structure for a school emergency.

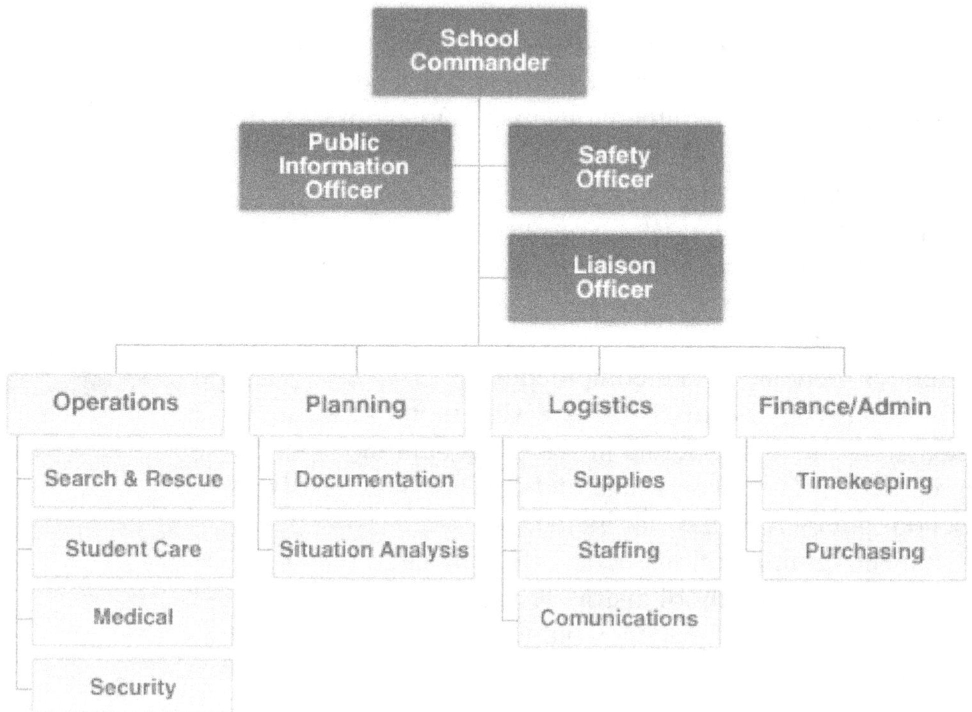

Tailoring ICS for Various Incidents

The following examples demonstrate how the ICS organization might change based on the incident:

- **ICS Structure for a Small Playground Incident:** For a playground incident involving one student injured, it probably would not be necessary to assign Section Chiefs for Logistics, Planning, or Finance/Administration. The principal or a teacher would act as the Incident Commander as well as the Operations Section Chief, and would coordinate with emergency medical services personnel to treat the student's injuries.

- **ICS Structure for a Fire Incident:** In the event of a complex fire at a school, command may be shared among more than one Incident Commander. For example an Incident Commander from the fire department would establish tactical objectives for fire suppression. A second Incident Commander representing the school may help ensure that student care needs are addressed in the decisionmaking process. If the fire is suspicious, a law enforcement representative may also be in the Command structure. This is referred to as Unified Command.

Using Unified Command

The Unified Command organization consists of multiple Incident Commanders from the various jurisdictions or agencies operating together to form a single command structure.

When implemented properly, Unified Command enables agencies with different legal, geographic, and functional responsibilities to coordinate, plan, and interact effectively.

In the case of a school incident, the role of the school Incident Commander may be limited to reunification, crisis counseling, and student care (shelter, feeding, and academic activities).

Covering All ICS Bases in the School Plan

A school's emergency operations plan should include procedures for each of the functional ICS areas, as well as for others that may be pertinent to the school.

Lesson 5 introduced the roles and responsibilities to include in your school EOP to address the ICS areas:

- Senior Executive (Superintendent, Principal, Emergency Management Official, Elected Official, etc.)
- Incident Commander
- Public Information Officer
- Liaison Officer
- Safety Officer
- Operations Section Chief
- Planning Section Chief
- Logistics Section Chief
- Finance and Administration Section Chief

Note: Your school EOP may need to address how ICS areas will be assigned with limited staff, for example if an incident occurs when school is over for the day.

Setting Up a Buddy System

Teachers assigned ICS positions may need to leave their classes to perform emergency functions during an incident. To ensure all students are supervised, your school may use a buddy system, pairing teachers of classrooms that are near each other.

For an effective buddy system:

- Class rosters should be accessible by the buddy teachers.
- Both classes should evacuate to the same location or go to the same safe area of the school.

Class rosters should be kept in a readily accessible location with other emergency supplies (e.g., whistle, pens, signs, flashlight, etc.).

Lesson Summary

This lesson presented information on incorporating ICS in your school's emergency operations plan.

The next lesson presents information on how to train, exercise, evaluate, and improve your school emergency operations plan.

Lesson 7: Training, Exercising, and Maintaining the Plan

Lesson Overview

After your plan is developed, you need to ensure staff and students are familiar with emergency procedures and have the knowledge, skills, and abilities to perform the tasks in the plan. You also need to keep your plan up to date.

This lesson addresses processes to ensure you train, exercise, and maintain your plan. At the completion of this lesson you should be able to:

- Explain the benefits of training and exercising the school emergency operations plan (EOP).
- Identify the types of exercises available to exercise the school's plan.
- Describe steps for developing effective exercises.
- Describe how exercise results are used to improve school preparedness efforts.

Implement and Maintain the Plan

The CPG planning process contributes to overall preparedness for your school as part of a continuous cycle of planning, organizing, equipping, training, exercising, evaluating, and improving.

Earlier lessons introduced the first five steps of the CPG planning process. This lesson reviews step 6, implement and maintain the plan. This step includes:

- Training,
- Exercising, and
- Reviewing, revising, and maintaining the plan.

Benefits of Training

Once the school plan has been approved, the next step is training. Training provides staff, students, parents, and other stakeholders with the knowledge, skills, and tools they need to perform procedures and critical tasks to respond during an emergency.

Benefits of training on the school EOP include:

- Enabling school personnel and students to respond rapidly and effectively in times of stress.
- Enhancing the school's preparedness capabilities.
- Familiarizing staff, students, parents, and other stakeholders with processes, policies, and procedures.
- Allowing staff, students, parents, and other stakeholders to acquire and retain the knowledge and skills needed to implement the school's EOP.

Types of Training

Because time and budgets are tight at schools, it may not be possible to provide all training in a traditional classroom environment. Consider delivering training in different ways depending on what needs to be conveyed:

- **Briefings:** Short meetings that provide information about a specific topic (e.g., new evacuation sites, tips on how to use the student information system to find student contact information, new district contact information).
- **Seminars/classroom training:** Used to introduce new programs, policies, or procedures. Provide information to students and staff on roles and responsibilities. This may also include training presented outside of the school (e.g., first aid, CERT).
- **Workshops:** Resemble a seminar but are employed to build specific products, such as a draft plan or policy.

Training, Then Exercising

Once you have conducted training, then you can begin to conduct exercises on the procedures in the EOP.

Exercises build on the knowledge acquired in the training to:

- Allow testing of emergency policies, plans, and procedures.
- Provide a safe environment to practice procedures using equipment and resources.
- Build relationships that result in better coordination and communication during an incident.

Benefits of Exercising the Plan

You've trained everyone. Now how do you know if the procedures in your EOP will work? Conduct exercises to . . .

- Assess and validate policies, plans, procedures, training, equipment, assumptions, and partnerships in a safe and controlled environment.
- Raise awareness of potential crisis situations.
- Clarify roles and responsibilities.
- Improve partnerships, coordination, and communication.
- Identify gaps in resources.
- Measure performance.
- Identify opportunities for improvement.

Planning Exercises

Your school planning team needs to identify what exercises to conduct and when.

- Begin with exercises that focus on a small part of the EOP, or on one specific procedure. Later add more complex exercises.
- Conduct exercises whenever new equipment is purchased or installed, or when new policies or procedures are developed.

Exercises determine how the plan worked, and do not focus on the performance of individuals.

Selecting Exercises

There are two main categories of exercises:

- Discussion-based exercises, which are used to familiarize personnel with procedures and policies. Facilitators lead the discussion and keep participants on track.
- Operations-based exercises, which are used to validate the plan. These exercises help clarify roles and responsibilities, identify gaps in resources, and improve performance. They include drills, functional exercises, and full-scale exercises.

Your school planning team selects the type of exercise based on what is to be validated, the training and exercises that have already been conducted, and available resources.

Tabletop Exercises

A tabletop exercise is a discussion-based activity in which a simulated scenario is presented and participants in the exercise respond as if the scenario were really happening. Tabletop scenarios are often based on actual incidents at the school or recent events in the news, particularly from neighboring communities or nearby States.

Tabletops:

- Involve key personnel and emergency responders.
- Allow participants to assess the plan and response procedures.
- Encourage participant discussions, problem solving, and decisionmaking in a low-stress environment.

Conducting Tabletops

To successfully conduct a tabletop exercise:

- Identify key participants for the exercise, such as school administrators and policy makers.
- Identify facilitator(s) to run the exercise, manage the information exchange, control the discussion, present scenario developments, and guide actions.
- Set exercise goals and objectives to lay out expectations for the exercise. Goals should be measurable and achievable.
- Outline an emergency incident to test a specific set of procedures, capability, and/or policy.
- Conduct a hot wash and a debrief to capture feedback and lessons learned.
- Develop a list of recommendations or an improvement plan to update training and exercise plans.

Drills

Drills are operations-based exercises that usually test a single specific operation or function within a single entity. Conducted in a realistic environment, drills are often used to test new policies or equipment, practice current skills, or prepare for larger scale exercises.

Conducting Drills

To successfully conduct a drill:

- Plans, policies, and procedures must be clearly defined and personnel must be familiar with them.
- Personnel must be trained on the processes and procedures to be drilled.
- It must be clear that a drill is being conducted, and that the situation is not an actual emergency.
- Evaluation and feedback must be included in the drill process.
- First responders should be included.

Using Drills for Simulated Emergencies

Drills can test how well faculty, staff, and students respond to simulated emergencies including:

- Bomb threats.
- Fire and/or explosion.
- Severe weather, such as a tornado.
- Intruder.
- HazMat incident, either originating inside or outside the school.
- Other incidents identified as hazards in your school EOP.

Using Drills To Exercise Procedures

Your school may conduct drills involving the entire population or just a classroom. Drills are used to test response procedures to ensure that students and staff understand what they are supposed to do—and can do it quickly in a simulated emergency. The following procedures can be exercised with a drill:

Evacuation Drills   WHEN THE ANNOUNCEMENT IS MADE:

1. Grab the emergency backpack on the way out of your room.
2. Take the closest and safest way out as posted.
3. Do not stop for student/staff belongings.
4. Go to the designated area and wait for instructions.
5. Check for injuries.

6. Take attendance. Hold up "GREEN" card if all are present. Report missing students to Command Post by holding up "RED" card. A runner will be sent to you.
7. If you have any other questions or problems, hold up your "RED" card.

Reverse Evacuation Drills

WHEN THE ANNOUNCEMENT IS MADE:

1. Move students/staff inside as quickly as possible.
2. Report to homeroom.
3. Take attendance. Use voice mail to report missing students.
4. Wait for further instructions.

Bus Evacuation Drills

WHEN THE ANNOUNCEMENT IS MADE:

1. Driver will notify dispatch with information about accident/incident including place of accident/incident and any injuries, and will tell them that he/she is evacuating the bus.
2. Driver will secure bus by putting on flashers, setting hand brake, turning engine off, and removing key.
3. Bus driver will announce the evacuation drill to students.
4. Driver must announce what kind of evacuation the students must do. Example: front door evacuation/back door evacuation, or split or side door evacuation.
5. Students must remain quiet, seated, and calm so that they can listen for directions.
6. No pushing or rushing when exiting bus.
7. Students must stay in single file to exit door.
8. Driver must direct students to a selected spot well away from the bus where students are to assemble and wait for the "all clear" signal.
9. Driver must do a head count before and after evacuation and check bus to assure that bus is empty.
10. After driver is assured that bus is empty, driver must secure the bus using chock blocks and emergency triangles and take the medical box with him/her.
11. Driver will join students after securing bus to take attendance of the students who were on the bus. Driver will stay with students until emergency,

medical, school, and contractor personnel arrive. Attendance list must be given to school personnel on duty.

Lockdown Drills

WHEN THE ANNOUNCEMENT IS MADE:

1. Students should report to the nearest classroom.
2. Close all windows, lock doors, and do not leave for any reason.
3. Cover all room and door windows.
4. Stay away from all doors and windows, and move students to interior walls and drop.
5. Shut off lights.
6. BE QUIET!
7. Wait for further instructions.

Shelter-in-Place Drills

WHEN THE ANNOUNCEMENT IS MADE:

1. Clear students from the halls immediately. Students should report to assigned classrooms.
2. Close and tape all windows and doors, and seal the gap between the bottom of the door and the floor.
3. Take attendance. Use voice mail to report missing students.
4. Do not allow anyone to leave the classroom. Allow emergency bathroom use only, using the buddy system.
5. Stay away from all doors and windows.
6. Permit classroom use of telephones in emergencies only.
7. Wait for further instructions.

Drop, Cover, and Hold Drills

WHEN THE COMMAND "DROP" IS GIVEN:

1. DROP: Take cover under a nearby desk or table, and face away from the window.
2. COVER your eyes by leaning your face against your arms.
3. HOLD on to the table or desk legs.

Functional Exercises

A functional exercise is the simulation of an emergency event that:

- Involves various levels of school, school district, and emergency management personnel.
- Involves trained personnel "acting out" their actual roles.
- Evaluates both the internal capabilities and responses of the school, school district, and emergency management officials.
- Evaluates the coordination activities between the school, school district, and emergency management personnel.

Full-Scale Exercise

A full-scale exercise is a multiagency, multijurisdictional, multidiscipline operations-based exercise involving functional (e.g., Joint Field Office, emergency operations center) and "boots on the ground" response (e.g., firefighters decontaminating mock victims).

To test the EOP using functional or full-scale exercises, schools may wish to inquire about upcoming community-wide exercises. In addition to exercising specific procedures and policies, these large-scale exercises can provide schools with an opportunity to test how their school EOP fits into the community EOP.

Developing Exercises

Now that you know the different ways your school can exercise the emergency operations plan, let's look at the how to develop exercises.

| Step 1. Assemble an exercise team |
| Step 2. Select the exercise type |
| Step 3. Develop exercise objectives |
| Step 4. Select exercise players |
| Step 5. Develop the exercise |
| Step 6. Conduct the exercise |

Planned, developed, and conducted correctly, exercises can be invaluable tools for preparing staff, testing the EOP, reinforcing concepts in the school EOP, and identifying areas for improvement. Exercises can also help planners identify coordination problems, operational issues, and emergency policy questions.

Evaluating Exercises

The last step in the exercise process is evaluating results. It is important to build in evaluation when you develop your exercise. Your exercise plan should include observing and recording exercise activities, comparing the performance of the participants against the objectives, and identifying strengths and weaknesses.

Evaluation and a debriefing should be conducted after every exercise and include:

- A hot wash, or debrief, which provides participants with the opportunity to evaluate themselves.
- A debriefing for facilitators and evaluators, which includes reviewing evaluations and hot wash notes.

Using Exercise Results

Exercise results are used to:

- Evaluate the EOP and identify deficiencies and lessons learned.
- Plan future training and exercises.
- Revise school EOP, policies, and procedures.
- Identify resource requirements.
- Identify training needs.
- Document the overall effectiveness of an exercise.

Lesson Summary

This lesson emphasized the importance of training and exercising as part of overall preparedness. Training and exercising can help you assess your school's emergency operations plan and provide input for making improvements based on exercise results.

You have now completed all of the lessons. The course summary includes a review of key concepts and the posttest.

www.ingramcontent.com/pod-product-compliance
Lightning Source LLC
Chambersburg PA
CBHW081021260726
48662CB00025B/2670